UNITED TWEETS of AMERICA

by Hudson Talbott

PUFFIN BOOKS
An Imprint of Penguin Group (USA)

P9-BZJ-317

Alaska

SD

ND

MT

IA

MN

WI

MI

NE

IL

IN

OH

AK

ID

Washington

Oregon

Montana

North Dakota

WY

Idaho

South Dakota

Wyoming

Nebraska

WA

Nevada

Utah

Colorado

Kansas

OR

CA

California

Arizona

New Mexico

Oklahoma

NV

Texas

AZ

UT

CO

KS

Hawaii

HI

NM

OK

TX

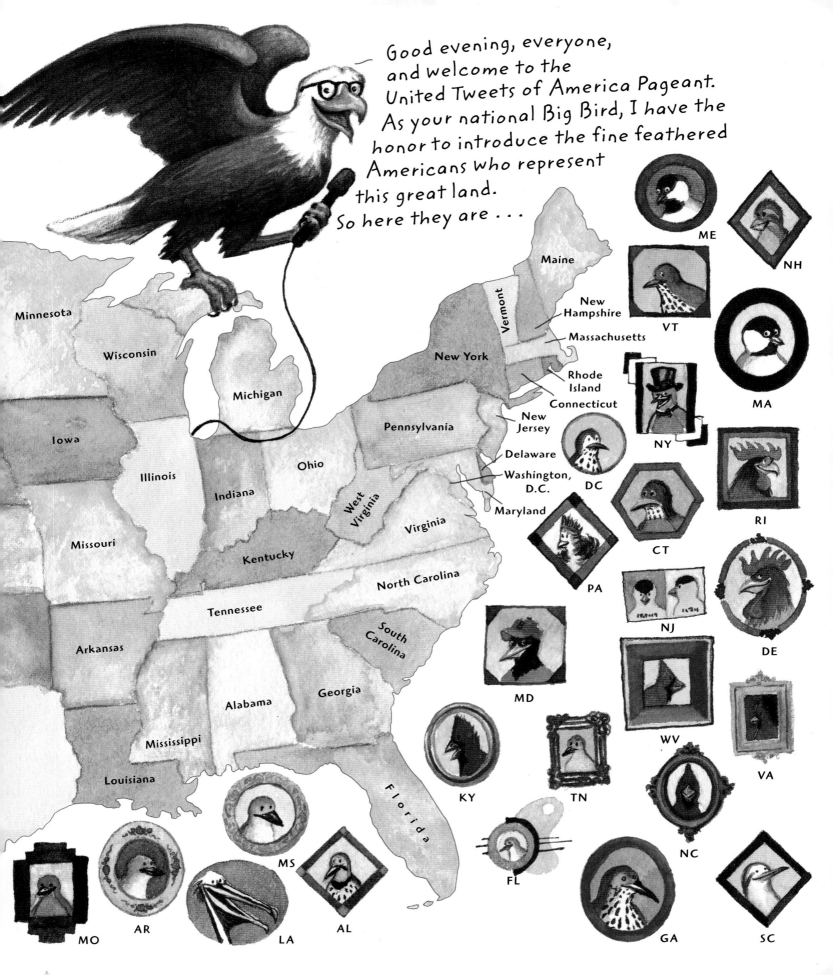

Good evening, everyone, and welcome to the United Tweets of America Pageant. As your national Big Bird, I have the honor to introduce the fine feathered Americans who represent this great land. So here they are . . .

—Move it
ALOHA! . . . ALOHA . . . ALO-HA . . . Aloha . . .
You're too slow
What's your problem?

LADIES AND GENTLEMEN,
THE PARADE OF STATES!
From Alabama to Wyoming,
each one is a winner . . .

And now we'll tell you
a little something about
each bird and the state
they call home.

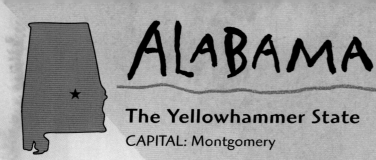

ALABAMA

The Yellowhammer State
CAPITAL: Montgomery

'Scuse me, y'all—
I'm a-huntin' for
some state bugs....

COOL ALABAMIANS:
Rosa Parks, Jesse Owens,
Hank Aaron, Nat "King" Cole,
Emmylou Harris, Helen Keller,
Coretta Scott King, Harper Lee

The Yellowhammer

(or Northern Flicker)
Since folks down here are not fond of the word *northern*, they
prefer to call their woodpecker the yellowhammer, after the Alabama soldiers
in the Civil War who wore uniforms with yellow trim and "hammered" the Yankees.
They even use the nickname for the whole state.

Alabama is also called the Heart of Dixie, which is the region south of the Mason-Dixon Line.

ALASKA
The Last Frontier
CAPITAL: Juneau

The Big Dipper and the North Star are on the Alaska state flag.

Hey, Woodpecker! I'm changing for the talent competition!

STATE SPORT: dog mushing

STATE FLOWER: no one seems to remember, possibly the forget-me-not

COOL ALASKAN: Joe Juneau— he came to Alaska in 1880 and discovered gold. They named the capital after him.

The Willow Ptarmigan

(the *P* is silent)

Changing color with the season, the willow ptarmigan turns white in winter to blend in with the snow and rusty brown in summer to blend in with the landscape. For a bird, he's quite a chameleon!

Alaska is also known as the Land of the Midnight Sun, because for a period of time during the summer, the sun does not set.

Alaska is the largest state by far, equal to 11 Alabamas or 425 Rhode Islands.

WINTER

SUMMER

ARIZONA

The Grand Canyon State
CAPITAL: Phoenix

Are you mocking me?
Why, I oughta . . .

The Cactus Wren

The cactus wren builds her nest in cacti to protect
her eggs from egg-eating rattlesnakes.
Small bird. Loud voice.

STATE PLANT: saguaro cactus

STATE FLOWER: saguaro cactus flower

STATE GEM: turquoise

STATE NECKWEAR: bolo tie

COOL ARIZONANS: Geronimo, Linda Ronstadt, Cochise, Cesar Chavez

ARKANSAS

The Natural State

CAPITAL: Little Rock

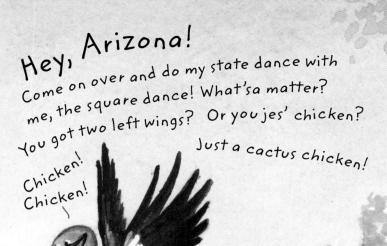

Hey, Arizona!
Come on over and do my state dance with me, the square dance! What'sa matter? You got two left wings? Or you jes' chicken?

Chicken! Chicken!

Just a cactus chicken!

STATE FLOWER: apple blossom

The Northern Mockingbird

The northern mockingbird mimics or "mocks" the calls of other birds in his range, sometimes all day and all night. (But most of his calls are rather uncalled for.)

STATE INSECT: honeybee

FAMOUS ARKANSANS:

Bill Clinton, Johnny Cash, Scott Joplin, Sam Walton, Al Green, Conway Twitty

STATE INSTRUMENT: fiddle

STATE VEGGIE: pink tomato

The town of Stuttgart is home to the World Championship Duck-Calling Contest.

CALIFORNIA

The Golden State

CAPITAL: Sacramento

The California Quail

The California quail is a member of the partridge family. (After starring in the hit TV series *The Partridge Family*, her career went south. She hopes the Top Tweet contest will help it take off again.)

And I'd like to thank the academy and the people of California for this award . . . and my stylist, Pepe, for my new 'do . . . but it's an honor just to be nominated . . .

California has the highest point (Mount Whitney) and lowest point (Death Valley) in the continental U.S.

STATE FLOWER: California poppy

STATE MAMMAL: grizzly bear

STATE MARINE MAMMAL: gray whale

STATE TREE: giant sequoia (*Sequoiadendron giganteum*)

STATE MOTTO: EUREKA! (Greek for "I found it!"; a term made famous during the California gold rush)

COLORADO

The Centennial State
CAPITAL: Denver

Colorado Springs is the home of the U.S. Air Force Academy.

The view from Pikes Peak inspired poet Katharine Lee Bates to write "America the Beautiful."

The Lark Bunting

The lark bunting looks like any sparrow much of the year, but during breeding season the male suits up in his black-and-white look when he's stylin' for the ladies.

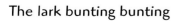

The lark bunting bunting

The lark bunting hunting

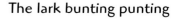

The lark bunting punting

CONNECTICUT

The Constitution State
CAPITAL: Hartford

Yankee Doodle went to town,
followed by a chicken,
if that bird won't shut his beak,
he's gonna get a lickin'.

STATE SONG: "Yankee Doodle"

STATE INSECT: praying mantis

STATE FLOWER: mountain laurel

STATE TREE: charter oak

The American Robin

The robin was named after an English bird by the early colonists.
Our robin eats good, solid American worms, believes in family values
(raising two or three broods a year) and never misses a Patriots game.

DELAWARE

The First State
CAPITAL: Dover

cluck
cluck
...and I love your little patriotic theme,
but, you know, we were the FIRST patriots!

Delaware is the FIRST state
because we signed
the Constitution first,
so we're number one!
We're number one!
We're number one!
cluck
cluck

cluck
cluck
cluck
cluck
cluck

...and you know my
talent already—
it's **crowing!**

But I think they
should call it
"**roostering.**"

Why crow?
Crows don't even
have a state ...

cluck cluck
cluck
cluck

cluck
cluck
And can you believe
these tail feathers?
They're my natural color!
Which reminds me, did you
hear that Rhode Island "Red"
is really gray? Maybe we should
call her the little red HENNA!
I wonder if the judges know ...

The Blue Hen Chicken

The blue hen chicken became a symbol for the Revolutionary War soldiers
from Delaware, who took their roosters along with them when they went to war.
When it came to fighting, they weren't chickens.

DISTRICT of COLUMBIA

Also known as Washington, D.C.

My home is the nation's capital!

OFFICIAL SONG:
"The Star-Spangled Banner"

OFFICIAL FLOWER:
The American Beauty Rose

D.C. is home to the
Library of Congress,
the largest library
in the world.

The Wood Thrush

The wood thrush scratched and pecked his way from field
to garden until reaching the lawns of power in the nation's capital.
(Although appointed for life as the District Bird, some in Congress are now calling for term limits.)

The Northern Mockingbird

Florida's mockingbird drives everyone crazy with his mocking, bragging and showing off. But the funny thing is that he's right about his home—by midwinter many of us can't wait to join him in the Sunshine State.

GEORGIA

The Peach State

CAPITAL: Atlanta

Georgia, Georrrrgia . . . the whole day through, just an old sweet song keeps Georgia on my mind . . .

Sing it, baby . . .

Oohhh-ooooohhh . . .

Oohhh-ooooohhh . . .

STATE SONG:

"Georgia on My Mind"

The Brown Thrasher

The brown thrasher is known for his rich variety of songs and beautiful voice.

OTHER GREAT SINGERS FROM GEORGIA: Ray Charles, Gladys Knight, Otis Redding, Little Richard, Jessye Norman, Brenda Lee, Amy Grant, Travis Tritt, Trisha Yearwood

Atlanta is the home of Coca-Cola, which was invented there in 1886.

A L O O O O H A A A A A !

HAWAII

The Aloha State

CAPITAL: Honolulu

The Nene

The nene is the rarest state bird. It was hunted to near extinction
until 1950, when there were only 30 birds left. In 1962 a hurricane struck
a small breeding facility, freeing several birds. They adapted to the wild
quickly and began breeding on their own. Today there are about 800 nenes.
(*Nene* is also a good word to know for Scrabble or crossword puzzles.)

Hawaii is made up of eight islands in the middle of the Pacific Ocean. It is the most
isolated population center on Earth. The closest land is California, 2,390 miles away.

Kilauea is the world's most active volcano.

IDAHO

The Gem State

CAPITAL: Boise

Whatever . . .

Honey, could you bring me that twig sometime before the snow flies?

The Mountain Bluebird

The female mountain bluebird takes charge of building the nest since the male is so busy defending their territory.

FAMOUS IDAHOANS WITH COOL NAMES:

Gutzon Borglum—sculptor of Mount Rushmore

Harmon Killebrew—baseball player

Picabo Street—skier

Sacajawea—Native American interpreter and guide

The Northern Cardinal

Cardinals are usually mild-mannered birds, except during the mating season
when the males can become very protective of their territory.

Illinois is called the Land of Lincoln
because Abraham Lincoln grew up here
before becoming the sixteenth president.

Chicago is home to the world's largest cookie
factory, Nabisco. In 1995 they produced over
16,000,000,000 Oreos.

INDIANA

The Hoosier State
CAPITAL: Indianapolis

Oh, honey, relax!
You're making a scene!

Mom, make him stop!
Everybody's looking!

The Northern Cardinal

When the male cardinal sings loudly to claim
his territory, the female often joins in with him,
though not always in harmony.

Indianans have been called Hoosiers for almost 200 years, but no one really knows why.
Some say it comes from "Who's here?" Others say it's from "Whose ear?" which early Hoosiers
sometimes said after a brawl, as in, "I found this on the floor last night—do you know whose ear it is?"

Hoosier favorite Hoosier?
SOME FAMOUS ONES: Larry Bird, Michael Jackson, David Letterman, Cole Porter, James Dean

American Goldfinch

The American Goldfinch

Goldfinches are the bird world's party animals. They fly like they're on a roller coaster,
change into bright colors for the "party season," and their call sounds like "po-ta-to-chip."

OTHER FAMOUS IOWA "PARTY ANIMALS":
Ashton Kutcher, Glenn Miller, Grant Wood,
John Wayne, and of course, Herbert Hoover

Speaking of animals,
there are approximately five hogs
for every human in Iowa.

KANSAS

The Sunflower State
CAPITAL: Topeka

The Western Meadowlark

The western meadowlark can become so lost in her own beautiful song that she forgets where she is.

♪ Oh, give me a home where the buffalo roam . . . . . . where are we? Toto! I don't think we're in Kansas anymore!

Trust me, we're still in Kansas, and I'm not Toto.

STATE FLOWER:
sunflower

STATE ANIMAL:
American buffalo

The Wizard of Oz,
by L. Frank Baum, begins in Kansas, where a twister carries Dorothy's house over the rainbow to the wonderful land of Oz.

STATE SONG:
"Home on the Range"

KENTUCKY

The Bluegrass State
CAPITAL: Frankfort

I'm often asked, "What makes those old Kentucky homes so special?" It's Kentucky bluegrass seed, of course! Great for lawn and garden, or perfect for serving at your next dinner party, or for just catching a quick snack on the fly! Kentucky bluegrass— ask for it by name.

100% GENUINE

KENTUCKY BLUE GRASS SEEDS 25 lbs.

KENTUCKY BLUE GRASS SEEDS 25 lbs. 100% GENUINE

The Northern Cardinal

The northern cardinal would be a standout anywhere, but he knows that nothing sets off his red color better than Kentucky's bluegrass.

STATE SONG: "My Old Kentucky Home" by Stephen Foster

COOL KENTUCKIANS: Daniel Boone, George Clooney, Abraham Lincoln, Muhammad Ali, Jefferson Davis, Diane Sawyer, the Judds, Loretta Lynn

UNOFFICIAL STATE BEVERAGE: mint julep

The Kentucky Derby in Louisville is the oldest and most important horse race in the world.

LOUISIANA

The Pelican State

CAPITAL: Baton Rouge
(French for "Red Stick")

Why, howdy, li'l chippa-dee-dee!
How 'bout droppin' in for some jambalaya?
It's like a Mardi Gras in your mouth!

The Brown Pelican

The brown pelican has an expandable throat pouch that he uses as a fishnet, sweeping up tasty treats. He is the largest state bird, and has a personality to match.

New Orleans is home to the nation's greatest party, Mardi Gras, and is also the birthplace of jazz.

The Black-Capped Chickadee

Chickadees deal with the harsh northern winters by storing away seed in holes and under tree bark.

MAINE
The Pine Tree State
CAPITAL: Augusta

Sorry, mista.
Gotta get the seed in 'fore the storm hits—
nor'easter a-coming!
But if ya need any lobstas,
just give a holla!

Maine supplies 90% of all lobsters consumed in the U.S. It also supplies 99% of the blueberries and 90% of the toothpicks.

MARYLAND

The Old Line State

CAPITAL: Annapolis

Hey, try a crab cake!

The Baltimore Oriole

Great bird. Great town. Great team.

FAMOUS BALTIMORE ORIOLES: Cal Ripken Jr., Billy Ripken, Jim Palmer, Brooks Robinson, and Luis Aparicio. The most famous baseball player of all time, Babe Ruth, began his career as an Oriole.

"The Star-Spangled Banner" was written by Marylander Francis Scott Key when he noticed a certain rocket's red glare coming from Fort McHenry in Baltimore Harbor.

MASSACHUSETTS

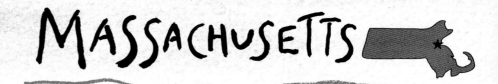

The Bay State
CAPITAL: Boston

The Black-Capped Chickadee

Chickadees are always ready for a free meal.
They have been getting them since the first Thanksgiving.

MICHIGAN

The Wolverine State

CAPITAL: Lansing

And he wonders why we call him a loon . . .

FLORIDA

The American Robin

Contrary to popular belief, not all robins go south for the winter. A few flocks will stay
close to their home range, eating berries until the worms wiggle awake in spring.

Detroit is called the Motor City, being the home of
the American automobile industry for over 100 years.

Michigan is also known as the Great Lakes State because it touches four of the five Great Lakes.
One of them is never more than 85 miles away from any point in Michigan.

MINNESOTA

Land of 10,000 Lakes

(actually, it's more like 12,000)

CAPITAL: Saint Paul

Hey, bud, could you give me a lift to to Lake Superior?

This place looks just like it from the air, but it's only the parking lot for the Mall of America.

The Loon

Loons spend most of their lives in the water and they
splash across its surface to become airborne. They sometimes mistake pavement for
a lake and then have trouble getting off the ground again.

INVENTED IN MINNESOTA: the snowmobile; Rollerblades; Snickers, Milky Way
and other Mars candy bars; canned ham; water skis; Scotch tape; the stapler;
the pop-up toaster; Wheaties; and the children's book section in libraries

The Mall of America is the largest mall in the U.S., equal in size to 78 football fields.

MISSISSIPPI

The Magnolia State

CAPITAL: Jackson

STATE FLOWER: the magnolia

Thankyouverymuch... and now I'd like to do a tune for a certain little someone in the front row.

I have red roses for a blue lady...

The Mockingbird

One of the greatest singers of all the state birds,
the mockingbird is known as the "King of Song."

OTHER MISSISSIPPI SONGBIRDS: Faith Hill, Leontyne Price, Muddy Waters, LeAnn Rimes,
Jimmy Buffett, Tammy Wynette, and the KING—Elvis Presley, born in Tupelo

...and, baby, I'm gonna make you a nest that will be the Taj Mahal of birds' nests!

MISSOURI

The Show Me State

CAPITAL: Jefferson City

Oh, yeah? Show me.

STATE TREE: flowering dogwood

The Eastern Bluebird

The male bluebird often flaps his wings above a nest site in order to attract a mate.

(But usually the female is left to build the nest herself.)

Missouri is called the Show Me State because a congressman once said, "I'm from Missouri, you'll have to show me," meaning he was hard to impress with words alone.

MONTANA

The Treasure State
CAPITAL: Helena

*Shove off, buddy!
You're messin' up
my aria!*

The Western Meadowlark

The western meadowlark is one of the most popular choices for state birds due to its melodious voice and enchanting personality.

MONTANA IS A BIG BIRD STATE:
10,000 tundra swans, 10,000 pelicans, 300,000 snow geese, the largest population of trumpeter swans in the lower 48 states and the largest population of nesting loons in the western U.S. make Montana their home for at least a portion of their year.

It also has the largest grizzly bear population in the lower 48 states and the largest migratory elk population in the U.S. The elk, deer and antelope populations each outnumber the humans.

Hey! That's MY song! Nobody sings that but ME!

NEBRASKA
The Cornhusker State
CAPITAL: Lincoln

The Western Meadowlark

The meadowlark is one of the most abundant birds of the North American grasslands but still prefers to sing alone. (Even birds can be divas.)

You folks care to make a little wager on who wins the singing contest?

Kool-Aid was invented in Hastings in 1927.

The world's largest porch swing seats 25 people and is located in Hebron.

STATE INSECT: honeybee

NEVADA

The Silver State
CAPITAL: Carson City

Nevada produces the most gold of any state, but California already won the title of the Golden State, so Nevada settled for the silver. (The bronze went to Romania.)

STATE REPTILE:
desert tortoise

OUT-OF-STATE REPTILE:
Texas horned toad

Las Vegas is the fastest-growing city in the U.S.

The Mountain Bluebird

Most studies of mountain bluebirds involve birds in nest boxes.
Little is known about their behavior in casinos.

NEW HAMPSHIRE

The Granite State
CAPITAL: Concord

They call that round thing the sun.

The Purple Finch

The purple finch is actually more of a rosy red, but winters in New Hampshire can make anybody turn purple.

STATE FLOWER: lilac
STATE FRUIT: pumpkin
STATE SPORT: skiing
STATE MOTTO: "Live free or die"

Giving their state a nickname was not a high priority for the people of New Hampshire. (In fact, it was taken for granite.)

New Jersey

The Garden State

CAPITAL: Trenton

New Jersey is the most densely populated state in the union. It also has the most highways per square mile of any state.

The American Goldfinch

The goldfinch can be spotted from a distance by the male's bright yellow summer plumage color and a flight pattern that looks as if he's weaving through traffic on the Jersey Turnpike.

NJ TURNPIKE 23
PARKWAY 17
US 78

PRINCETON

FAMOUS JERSEY CHIRPERS:

Jon Bon Jovi, Frank Sinatra, Dionne Warwick, Paul Robeson, Sarah Vaughn, and The Boss—Bruce Springsteen

NEW MEXICO

The Land of Enchantment

CAPITAL: Santa Fe

The Greater Roadrunner

The roadrunner lives on the ground and eats small animals and snakes. He has been clocked at over 18 miles per hour. (He does not say beep-beep.)

AWARD FOR COOLEST STATE FLAG:

The flag's design comes from the ancient Zia people and represents the sun with four sets of four rays coming out of its sides.

Enough about me—let's talk about my flag.

The flag's rays represent the four gifts of Life:

4 DIRECTIONS: north, south, east, west

4 SEASONS: spring, summer, fall, winter

4 TIMES OF DAY: dawn, noon, dusk, night

4 AGES: childhood, youth, adulthood, wisdom

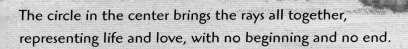

The circle in the center brings the rays all together, representing life and love, with no beginning and no end.

NEW YORK
The Empire State
CAPITAL: Albany

If I can make it there,
I'll make it anywhere—
it's up to you, New York, New York!

Out-of-towners . . .

Must be from upstate . . .

The Eastern Bluebird

With his bright colors and cheerful song, the bluebird often represents happiness.

New York is the center of the music world. It is home to the Metropolitan Opera, the New York City Opera, Broadway, Off-Broadway, Off-Off-Broadway and thousands of singer/actor/waiters.

NORTH CAROLINA

The Tar Heel State
CAPITAL: Raleigh

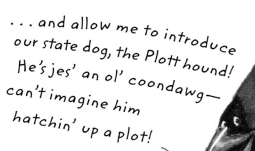

. . . and allow me to introduce
our state dog, the Plott hound!
He's jes' an ol' coondawg—
can't imagine him
hatchin' up a plot!

The Northern Cardinal

With his warm personality and juicy red color, the cardinal's many
fans find him hard to resist.

STATE DOG: the Plott hound

The Plott hound was bred by a family named Plott in the 1700s.
Although not well known elsewhere, it is still used for hunting
in the Tar Heel State.

TAR HEELS: It is believed that General Lee gave the North Carolinians this
nickname because he said they stuck to the battle like they had tar on their heels.

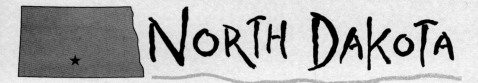

NORTH DAKOTA

The Peace Garden State
CAPITAL: Bismarck

The Western Meadowlark

The song of the meadowlark truly embodies the spirit of the American West.

YeeeeEEEEEEE-HAAAAAA!!!

STATE HORSE: the Nakota

Nakota horses are descended from the ponies of the great Sioux chief Sitting Bull. They roamed the prairies freely until just a few years ago, when the National Park Service rounded them up. Many people are working to save this special breed.

The International Peace Garden straddles the border between North Dakota and Canada.

OHIO

The Buckeye State
CAPITAL: Columbus

Ohio is the home state of Orville and Wilbur Wright, who invented and flew the first successful airplane, after studying the flight of birds.

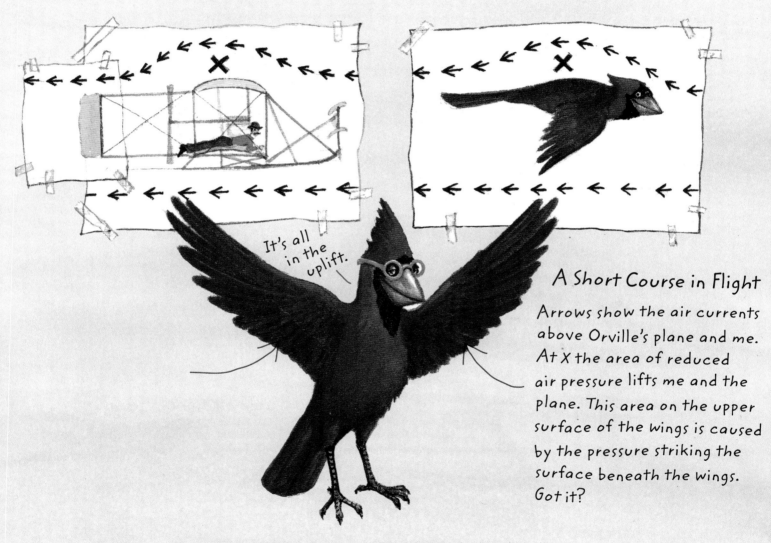

It's all in the uplift.

A Short Course in Flight

Arrows show the air currents above Orville's plane and me. At X the area of reduced air pressure lifts me and the plane. This area on the upper surface of the wings is caused by the pressure striking the surface beneath the wings. Got it?

The Northern Cardinal

Redbird is a foremost authority on flight and locating bird feeders.

Ohio is called the Buckeye State because many early settlers built log homes from trees that had nuts that resemble buck's eyes.

OKLAHOMA

The Sooner State
CAPITAL: Oklahoma City

AWARD FOR BEST STATE SONG: "OKLAHOMA!" by Rodgers and Hammerstein

We're only sayin' you're doin' fine, Oklahoma, OKLA-HOMA, OK!

STATE INSECT: OK! honeybee

STATE GAME ANIMAL: OK! whitetail deer

STATE GAME BIRD: OK! turkey

OK!

STATE REPTILE: OK! green lizard

STATE MAMMAL: OK! bison

STATE FURBEARING MAMMAL: OK! raccoon

The Scissortail Flycatcher

This multitalented bird catches insects in midair, does spectacular aerial displays and aggressively defends his territory when he's not singing show tunes.

Oklahomans are called Sooners. During the land rush of 1889, when people were allowed to race into open territories and claim land, some folks jumped the gun and got land **sooner** than others.

OREGON

The Beaver State

CAPITAL: Salem

AWARD FOR MOST UNIQUE STATE MOTTO:

"She flies with her own wings"

Not only that, but I lay my own eggs, sing my own tunes, have a movie deal for my life story, and my workout video is hitting stores next week!

She also toots her own horn.

STATE MASCOT AND COMMENTATOR:
the beaver

The Western Meadowlark

The western meadowlark seeks out places to perch where her melodic voice can be easily heard: fence posts, mailboxes and talk shows (but only when she has a new book to plug).

The Oregon Trail was one of the most important wagon train routes for early pioneers settling the West. Spanning over half the continent (2,170 miles), it began in Missouri and ended in Oregon. Most people walked the whole way. Except for the western meadowlark, who flew.

PENNSYLVANIA

The Keystone State
CAPITAL: Harrisburg

The Ruffed Grouse

The ruffed grouse is unique among the state birds for his impressive display rituals.

. . . and you should see what I do when we win the World Series!

Hershey is home to . . . guess!

Punxsutawney is home to Phil, the weather-predicting groundhog.

Can I go go back to bed now?

Pittsburgh was home of the world's first baseball stadium.

Philadelphia was home to:
• Sewing the first American flag
• Signing the Declaration of Independence
• Casting of the Liberty Bell

PENNSYLVANIA

KEYSTONE STATE

PHIL

Ah, but MY state makes displays for ME! Check this out . . .

 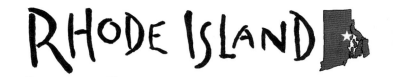

The Ocean State
(also known as Little Rhody)
CAPITAL: Providence

The Rhode Island Red

First bred in Little Compton, these chickens proved to be excellent for both eating and egg-laying. The breed quickly spread to farms everywhere and became a staple of the American poultry industry. A grateful and well-fed public erected a monument to "Red" in 1925. There are now special flocks of purebred Reds to ensure that the breed will never die out.

THE RHODE ISLAND RED

Rhode Island is not really an island but takes its name from an island in its large bay.

Rhode Island is the smallest state, but even though it is 47 miles long, it has 400 miles of coastline.

SOUTH CAROLINA

The Palmetto State
CAPITAL: Columbia

Hilton Head hop

The Carolina Wren

Carolina wrens mate for life, sing constantly and interweave their voices into one song. But that's nothing compared to what happens when they hit the dance floor.

leghold loop-di-loop

The shag is the official state dance of South Carolina. It is famous for its fancy footwork and broad variety of steps. The variation known as the Carolina Wren Shag also involves wing-flapping, beak-wagging, airborne displays and the ever-popular "death drop."

beak-tweak backflip

wing swing

beak-to-beak bebop

tail-feather tango

death drop

shoreline slide

And after shagging, most wrens enjoy the state's official beverage: sweet tea.

SOUTH DAKOTA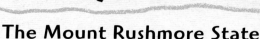

The Mount Rushmore State
CAPITAL: Pierre

Mount Rushmore is also called the Shrine of Democracy, and shows the faces of presidents Washington, Jefferson, Theodore Roosevelt, and Lincoln. They are over 60 feet high. Lincoln's nose is larger than the head of the Sphinx in Egypt.

As state birds we're expected to step up and be role models of leadership in our state. So that's why I've taken charge of renovating Mount Rushmore.

The Ring-Necked Pheasant

One of the few non-native state birds, ringnecks are native to China and were introduced to South Dakota and other states in 1898.

FAMOUS NATIVE SOUTH DAKOTANS WITH COOL NAMES:
Crazy Horse, Red Cloud, Sitting Bull, Rain-in-the-Face

Dakota, Lakota and Nakota are all tribes of the Sioux nation.

TENNESSEE

The Volunteer State
CAPITAL: Nashville

'Scuse me, but I'm the mockingbird here.

Hey, are you a-mockin' me?

You step over that line and I'll . . .

You better cut that out.

Yeah? You and what army?

The Northern Mockingbird

Defending his territory with a variety of calls, the northern mockingbird
can give as good as he gets.

Elvis Presley's home, Graceland, in Memphis,
is the second most visited home in the U.S.A.

They could go at this for days.

FAMOUS TENNESSINGERS:
Aretha Franklin, Dolly Parton, Minnie Pearl,
Tina Turner, Tennessee Ernie Ford

STATE AMPHIBIAN: Tennessee cave salamander

TEXAS

The Lone Star State
CAPITAL: Austin

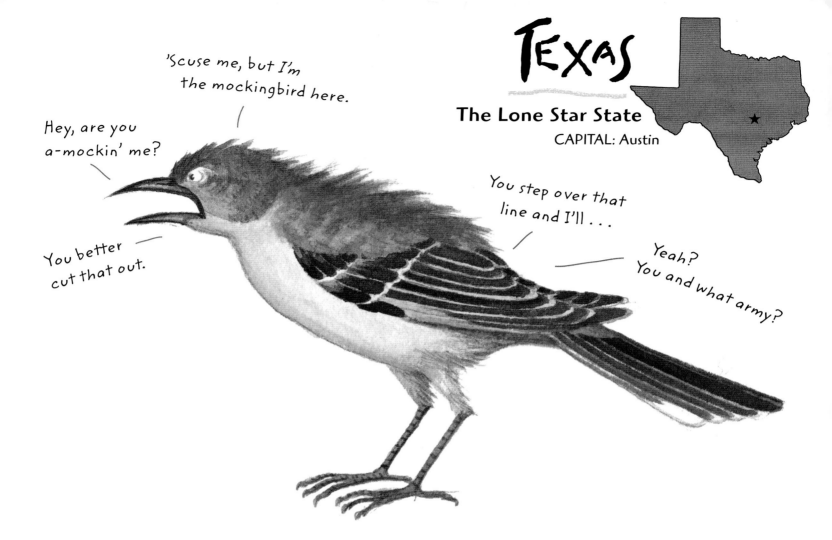

'Scuse me, but I'm the mockingbird here.

Hey, are you a-mockin' me?

You step over that line and I'll . . .

You better cut that out.

Yeah? You and what army?

The Northern Mockingbird

When they really get going, mockingbirds can imitate the sounds of a dog barking,
a cat yowling, a gate squeaking or even a lawnmower.

He's even worse when he sees a mirror.

STATE REPTILE: Texas horned lizard

Texas is the only state to have had the flags of
six different nations fly over it.

The largest ranch in the world,
the King Ranch, is in Texas and it is bigger
than the state of Rhode Island.

UtAH

The Beehive State
CAPITAL: Salt Lake City

Howdy, pardners!
You may be wonderin' what a
seagoin', sushi-eatin', West Coast
type dude like me is doin' here.
Well, that's a good story . . .

The California Gull

A Hero Bird's Story

In 1848 swarms of crickets were devouring the crops of the early Utah settlers
when suddenly huge flocks of gulls appeared and devoured the crickets.
In gratitude, the people built a monument to the birds and named
the California gull their state bird.

The country's first transcontinental railroad was completed at the Promontory Summit in Utah in 1869.

The town of Kanab is known as Little Hollywood because so many movies are shot there.

VERMONT

The Green Mountain State

CAPITAL: Montpelier

The Hermit Thrush

A shy bird, the hermit thrush's song is considered the most beautiful of all.

The name Vermont comes from the French words *vert,* meaning "green," and *mont,* for "mountain."

VIRGINIA

The Old Dominion State

CAPITAL: Richmond

Virginia is called the Mother of Presidents because more presidents have been born there than in any other state.

Hey! You can't claim him! We're his home state!

Thomas Jefferson

James Madison

William Henry Harrison

George Washington

James Monroe

Zachary Taylor

Woodrow Wilson

John Tyler

The Northern Cardinal

The male cardinal's constant push for more territory seems limitless, whether it's claiming a backyard, another state (seven isn't enough?) or the Father of Our Country.

WASHINGTON

The Evergreen State
CAPITAL: Olympia

You may've HAD Washington, but we ARE Washington.

STATE MAMMAL:
orca

STATE INSECT:
green darner
fly

STATE TREE:
spruce

George Washington

Your
ad
here

Space Needle

STATE FRUIT:
apple

Starbucks

The American Goldfinch

The goldfinch's song can vary from region to region. (The Washington goldfinch,
for example, sounds like "dot-com-dot-com-dot-com.")

WEST VIRGINIA

The Mountain State

CAPITAL: Charleston

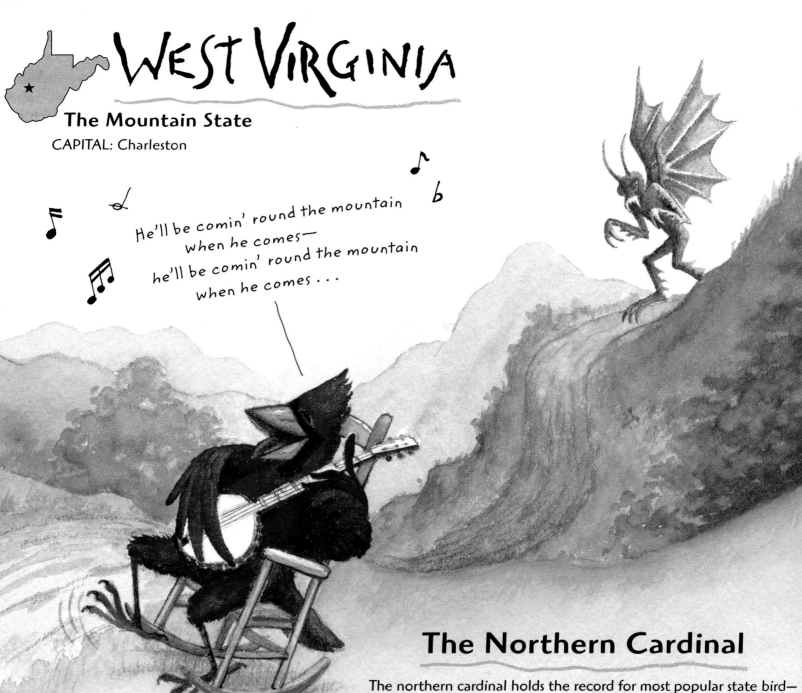

He'll be comin' round the mountain when he comes—
he'll be comin' round the mountain when he comes . . .

The Northern Cardinal

The northern cardinal holds the record for most popular state bird—representing seven states. Try naming them without looking (hint: they each touch at least one other cardinal state).

MOTHMAN

Since the 1960s there have been many sightings of a strange creature with huge wings and bright red eyes. He came to be known as Mothman. A movie was even made featuring him.

The longest serving U.S. senator is West Virginia's Robert Byrd. At 88 years old, he was elected in 2006 to a record ninth term.

In 1947, West Virginian Chuck Yeager was the first human to fly faster than the speed of sound.

WISCONSIN

The Badger State

CAPITAL: Madison

You're sure-as-heck, gosh-darn welcome here, you betcha!

Where Cheeseheads ride Harleys!
(unofficial state motto)

The American Robin

When robins flock together for their big southward migration, their Harleys can be deafening. The Wisconsin flock calls itself Heck's Angels.

Milwaukee is the home of Harley-Davidson motorcycles.

Monroe is the Swiss Cheese Capital of the U.S.A.

Willows is Barbie's fictional hometown.

Bloomer is the Rope-Jumping Capital of the World.

Green Bay is the Toilet Paper Capital of the World.

Sheboygan is the Bratwurst Capital of the World.

Eagle River is the Snowmobile Capital of the World.

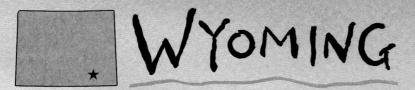

WYOMING

The Equality State
CAPITAL: Cheyenne

The Western Meadowlark

His cheerful singing and jackaloping skills have earned Westy
more state titles than any other bird in the West.

Rodeo is the state sport
of Wyoming.

Ride 'im, birdboy!

The jackalope is legendary
throughout the western U.S., but
Douglas, Wyoming, is the center of jackalope lore.
An eight-foot bronze jackalope statue graces its town square.
Little scientific information is known about this rare animal,
but it is thought to be a cross between an antelope and a killer jackrabbit.

AMERICA, GRACE ON THEE, THY GOOD WITH BIRDYHOOD TO SHINING SEA!

Hey, like we say in Kentucky, united we stand, divided we fall . . . and right now, I really mean it!

For Rudie,

the wind beneath my wings

PUFFIN BOOKS
Published by the Penguin Group
Penguin Group (USA) LLC
375 Hudson Street
New York, New York 10014

USA * Canada * UK * Ireland * Australia
New Zealand * India * South Africa * China

penguin.com
A Penguin Random House Company

First published in the United States of America by G. P. Putnam's Sons, a division of Penguin Young Readers Group, 2008
Published by Puffin Books, an imprint of Penguin Young Readers Group, 2015

Copyright © 2008 by Hudson Talbott

Penguin supports copyright. Copyright fuels creativity, encourages diverse voices, promotes free speech, and creates a vibrant culture. Thank you for buying an authorized edition of this book and for complying with copyright laws by not reproducing, scanning, or distributing any part of it in any form without permission. You are supporting writers and allowing Penguin to continue to publish books for every reader.

THE LIBRARY OF CONGRESS HAS CATALOGED THE G. P. PUTNAM'S SONS EDITION AS FOLLOWS:
Talbott, Hudson. United tweets of America / Hudson Talbott. p. cm.
ISBN 978-0-399-24520-6 (hc)
1. U.S. states—Miscellanea—Juvenile literature. 2. United States—Miscellanea—Juvenile literature.
3. State birds—United States—Juvenile literature. I. Title.
E180.T35 2008 973—dc22 2007019419

Puffin Books ISBN 978-0-14-751557-5

1 3 5 7 9 10 8 6 4 2